Polar Bears

Published by Wildlife Education, Ltd.
12233 Thatcher Court, Poway, California 92064
contact us at: 1-800-477-5034
e-mail at: animals@zoobooks.com
visit us at: www.zoobooks.com

ISBN 0-937934-85-2

Contents

The **polar bear** is King of the North. It reigns over a world of snow, ice, and water, where most animals cannot survive. There are other animals that live here also, such as seals, walruses, foxes, and geese. But the biggest, strongest, and fiercest of them all is the polar bear.

Among land animals, the polar bear is the largest predator in the world. Standing on its rear legs, it is tall enough to look an elephant in the eye! The biggest polar bear ever measured was a male that stood more than 11 feet tall and weighed 2,210 pounds. An average male weighs 1,000 pounds, and females weigh about half that much.

Despite their enormous size, polar bears are graceful and athletic. They jump over cracks in the ice more than 20 feet wide. They climb snow banks and steep ridges of ice. They are also expert long-distance swimmers, and are often seen in the Arctic Ocean several miles from shore.

Polar bears look like other bears, except for a few distinct differences. They have narrower heads, smaller ears, and longer teeth than other bears, and their hair structure gives them their own solar heating. In these and other ways, polar bears are built to live and hunt in the frozen Arctic.

Most of a polar bear's life is spent hunting for food. Its favorite food is seal blubber. A polar bear wanders far and wide in its search for seals. Yet even when it finds them, they aren't easy to catch. This bear uses many different techniques to hunt seals. But most often, the seals get away, and the polar bear must continue its lonely search.

Polar bears live and hunt alone, except when they are cubs. It takes about three years before a young polar bear is big enough to live and hunt without its mother. Once it is fully grown, a polar bear is safe from almost anything—except other polar bears and humans. If they escape these dangers, polar bears can live long lives. A polar bear once lived in the London Zoo for 41 years.

Polar bears live at the top of the world. This icy region from the North Pole to the northern coasts of Europe, Asia, and North America is called the Arctic. Most of the Arctic is ocean, and much of it is covered with ice.

Polar bears usually live on the ice. They use it as a platform for stalking seals. But the amount of ice in the ocean changes from summer to winter, so the polar bears must migrate. Most of them travel to the same summer and winter areas year after year.

Polar bears do not always travel over land or ice. They are strong swimmers and can easily swim up to 60 miles without stopping to rest.

The summer and winter ranges of polar bears are shown by the yellow areas on the maps below. In the summer, the ice in the southern part of the Arctic Ocean melts. Most polar bears travel north to stay on the ice. Because there is not enough ice for them all, some polar bears head south to spend the summer on land.

In the winter and spring, ice forms over most of the Arctic Ocean. Polar bears come down from the north to hunt on this new ice. And those living on shore go north for the same reason.

NORTH POLE

ARCTIC OCEAN

SUMMER RANGE

NORTH POLE

ARCTIC OCEAN

WINTER RANGE

Polar bears live on ice, but only where they can find seals. For example, the area nearest the North Pole is covered with a solid sheet of ice **1**. But very few seals live this far north, so you won't find many polar bears here either.

Farther south, the ice breaks into huge "islands" **2**. This is where most seals live, and most polar bears too. Every bear has a hunting territory, shown here as the dark orange area in the middle. If it can't find enough seals in its own territory, the polar bear will wander over a larger area, as shown in light orange.

Ice also forms along the shorelines in the winter **3**. This is where most female seals come to have their babies. And in early spring, many polar bears come here to hunt for seals.

When they migrate, polar bears often travel hundreds of miles. But they usually return each year to the same areas where they learned to hunt as young cubs.

In summer, when the ice melts, some polar bears come ashore. For a few months, they act just like brown bears, staying in the forests and eating wild berries.

Mother polar bears and their cubs usually spend the winter in dens on land. In the spring, they return to the ice to hunt seals. This mother is teaching her cubs to hunt.

9

The body of a polar bear is made for living in the cold. In fact, polar bears like the cold. They are so good at staying warm that they get uncomfortable even on slightly warm days. For one thing, polar bears have large bodies. And large bodies usually hold heat much better than small bodies. The large body of a polar bear also has extra layers of protection against the cold.

The body of a polar bear has many features that help make it an excellent hunter. Unlike other bears, polar bears get most of their food by hunting, because there aren't many plants to eat where polar bears live. Polar bears are extremely powerful.

QUESTION: Of the two outfits shown at right, which one would keep you warmest in a cold wind? Which one would be best for keeping you warm in the water?

ANSWER: A parka would keep you nice and warm in the cold wind.

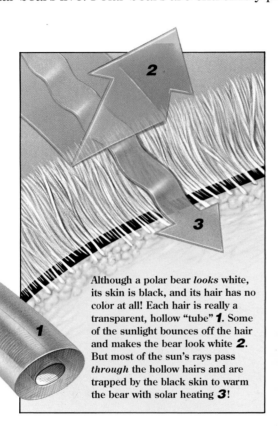

Although a polar bear *looks* white, its skin is black, and its hair has no color at all! Each hair is really a transparent, hollow "tube" **1**. Some of the sunlight bounces off the hair and makes the bear look white **2**. But most of the sun's rays pass *through* the hollow hairs and are trapped by the black skin to warm the bear with solar heating **3**!

Fur

Skin

Blubber

A polar bear's front paws are its most dangerous weapons. Each one is like a 25-pound sledgehammer that the bear can swing with deadly force. The paw is also a "handy" tool. The large rough pad keeps the bear from slipping on the ice. The short, sharp claws are just right for holding on to slippery prey.

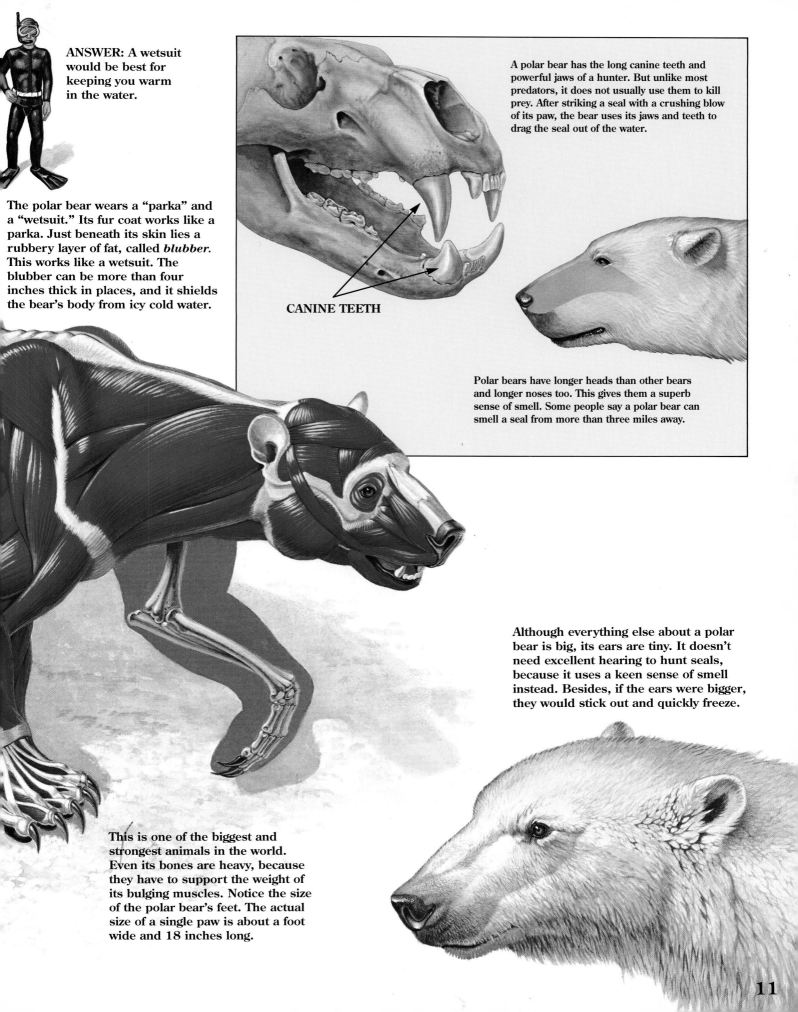

ANSWER: A wetsuit would be best for keeping you warm in the water.

The polar bear wears a "parka" and a "wetsuit." Its fur coat works like a parka. Just beneath its skin lies a rubbery layer of fat, called *blubber*. This works like a wetsuit. The blubber can be more than four inches thick in places, and it shields the bear's body from icy cold water.

A polar bear has the long canine teeth and powerful jaws of a hunter. But unlike most predators, it does not usually use them to kill prey. After striking a seal with a crushing blow of its paw, the bear uses its jaws and teeth to drag the seal out of the water.

CANINE TEETH

Polar bears have longer heads than other bears and longer noses too. This gives them a superb sense of smell. Some people say a polar bear can smell a seal from more than three miles away.

Although everything else about a polar bear is big, its ears are tiny. It doesn't need excellent hearing to hunt seals, because it uses a keen sense of smell instead. Besides, if the ears were bigger, they would stick out and quickly freeze.

This is one of the biggest and strongest animals in the world. Even its bones are heavy, because they have to support the weight of its bulging muscles. Notice the size of the polar bear's feet. The actual size of a single paw is about a foot wide and 18 inches long.

11

*H*unting on ice is not easy. And catching expert swimmers like seals is even harder. To catch them, a polar bear needs a keen sense of smell, a variety of hunting methods, and incredible patience.

A polar bear may have to walk or swim several miles just to find seals. Then it may find them lying on the ice, swimming in open water, or even swimming under the ice.

Wherever seals are, the polar bear must be prepared to hunt them. During certain times of the year, hunting is fairly easy. At other times it is very difficult.

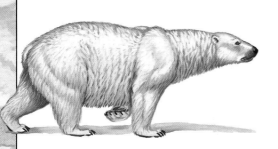

In the spring, when seals are easiest to find, most polar bears eat so much they may gain more than 200 pounds! Storing fat lets them use this reserve of nutrition later in the year, when hunting is not so easy.

In fall and winter, the polar bear is forced to diet because seals are harder to find, so the bear doesn't have as much to eat. Now it uses its stored fat. By late winter, the formerly fat bear has become a skinny bear.

SNOW GOOSE

When polar bears can't find seals, they may try hunting other animals. They sometimes hunt snow geese, and they have been seen feeding on *belugas*, or white whales.

BELUGA

LEMMING

A polar bear will even hunt this tiny lemming. Think how strange it must look to see an 800-pound bear pouncing on a 2-ounce rodent.

With its keen sense of smell, a polar bear sniffs out a seal's *birth lair*—a den under the snow, where seals have their babies. By spring, three or four feet of ice and snow may cover the lair. The polar bear pounces on the roof until it caves in, then plunges headfirst into the lair to capture the seals inside.

Sitting and waiting is the polar bear's most common method of hunting. It sits patiently beside a hole in the ice, where it knows a seal will come up for air. It may wait for hours, but must be alert when the seal appears. Then, with lightning speed, the bear slaps the seal with a gigantic paw and pulls the seal through the breathing hole.

A polar bear can also sneak up on a seal by *crawling*. It lies flat on the ice and creeps slowly toward the seal.

Occasionally, a polar bear attacks from the water. First, it swims noiselessly toward the seal.

When it gets close, the bear dives and approaches underwater. At the last second, it springs to the surface and lunges at the surprised seal.

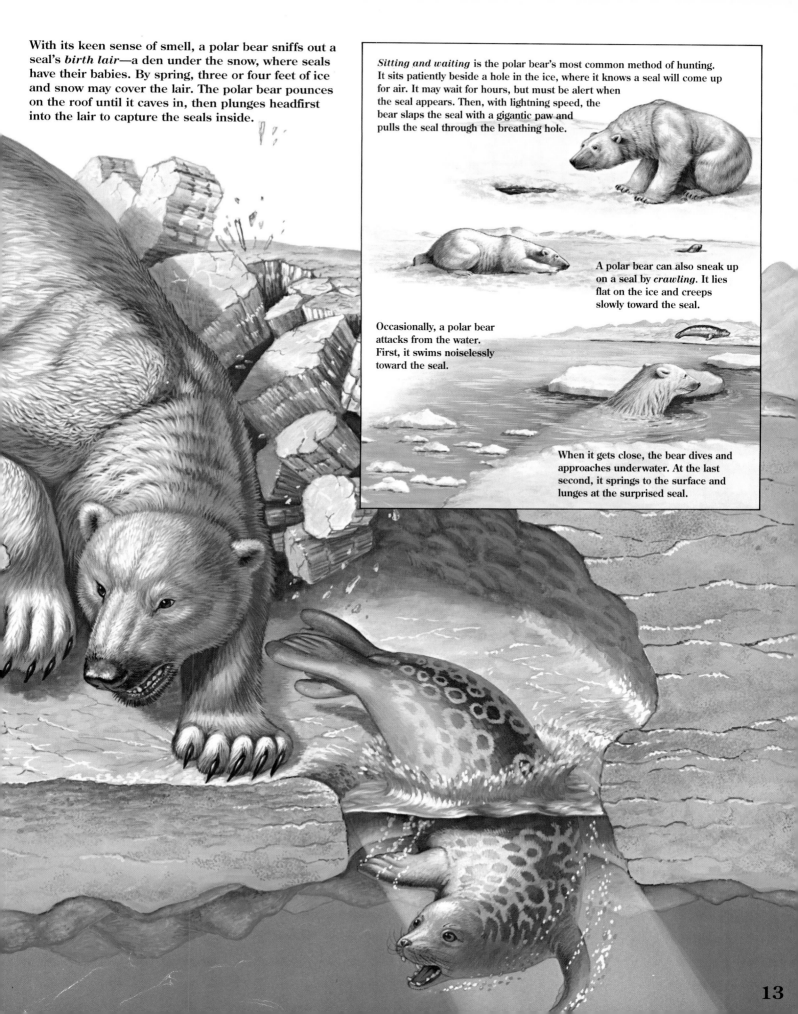

13

Polar bear cubs stay with their mothers until they are almost three years old. During that time, the mother is as devoted and loyal as any mom can be. She finds food for them. She teaches them to hunt. She protects them, and she defends them with her own life, if necessary.

A mother polar bear usually gives birth to two cubs in the middle of winter. At birth, the cubs are incredibly tiny. For three months, they must stay inside a warm den under the snow, where the mother gives them milk and keeps them warm.

A den dug out of the snow keeps mother and babies warm all winter long. To help keep out the cold, the den has a long entrance tunnel. The mother often builds a mound of snow in front of the tunnel to block the wind.

Imagine how much growing a baby polar bear has to do! At birth, it weighs about one pound and is small enough to hold in your hands. It cannot see or hear, and it has only a thin coat of white hair.

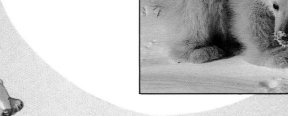

When a cub is three months old, it is finally ready to leave the den. But for several weeks, the little bear will hardly leave its mother's side.

In the first month, a cub grows more than four times its original size. By the time it is a month old, it can see and hear, but it still cannot walk.

One month old

A two-month-old cub weighs about as much as a newborn human. By this time, the cub knows how to walk, but it is still not strong enough to leave the den.

16

Young cubs may climb on their mother's back when they are frightened by a walrus, a human, or even another polar bear. Anything that threatens the cubs must face an angry mother. Female polar bears fight with every ounce of their strength to protect their cubs.

A mother polar bear is a gentle giant. This mother sits patiently while her cub gets a drink of milk. Then she naps while junior plays on her back.

Cubs remain with their mothers until they are almost fully grown. Even then, they love to play. In preparation for adulthood, they wrestle and lunge at one another in mock battles. The playful young bear peeking over the rock seems about to pounce on his mother as if she were a seal.

We have much to learn about the ways of polar bears. Until recently, few scientists traveled to the Arctic to study them in the wild. People used to think that adult polar bears didn't like one another's company. When seen together, they always seemed to be fighting. Now we know much of their fighting is just for fun. As we learn more about polar bears and their variety of behaviors, our fascination with them grows.

A polar bear often stands on its rear legs to look around and sniff the air. This behavior is natural to polar bears and is not just a trick they are taught in zoos and circuses.

Polar bears spend most of their time alone. When they tire of wandering over the ice to hunt for seals, they may sit for a short rest or curl up for a nap.

When polar bears meet, they greet each other by clasping muzzles. Afterward, they may wrestle and play for hours. A favorite wrestling place is in the water.

Polar bears have a tremendous curiosity—especially when they smell food. That is why so many of them visit the dump grounds in towns and villages throughout the Arctic. Some town dumps have become favorite sites for scientists to observe polar bears.

Cubs stay with their mothers for more than two years. Young cubs keep close to their mothers. Cubs a year old will range farther away and perhaps hunt, but they keep their eyes on mom. When they are two years old, the cubs may distance themselves by a mile or more, searching on their own for a seal's lair.

Hunting the polar bear used to be the truest test of a man's courage. With the help of his dogs and armed only with a spear, the hunter faced the great white bear. After his dogs cornered the bear, the hunter attacked with his spear. A ceremony lasting several days honored the spirit of the polar bear after the hunt.

The People of the North, or Inuit, have lived near polar bears for thousands of years. They have hunted polar bears, and they have also learned from them. Legend tells that these early nomadic hunters learned how to hunt seals and how to stay warm in the ice and snow of the frozen north by imitating polar bears.

Today the Inuit use modern tools and vehicles and live in modern houses. But many of them have kept alive the same respect for the polar bear that their ancestors had.

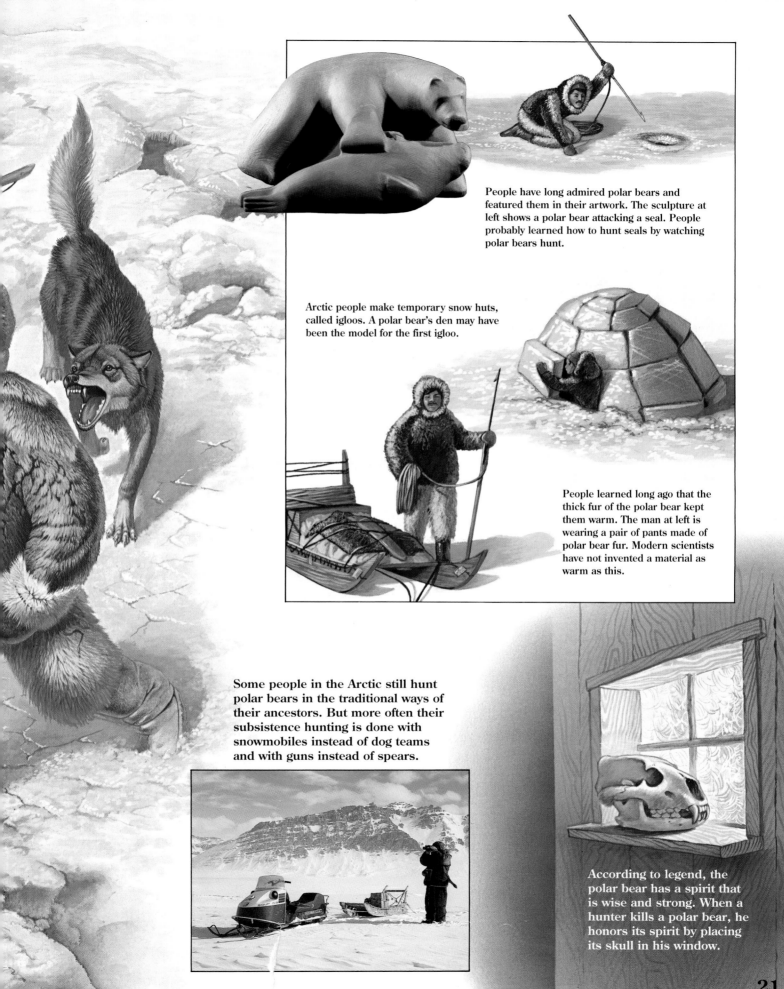

People have long admired polar bears and featured them in their artwork. The sculpture at left shows a polar bear attacking a seal. People probably learned how to hunt seals by watching polar bears hunt.

Arctic people make temporary snow huts, called igloos. A polar bear's den may have been the model for the first igloo.

People learned long ago that the thick fur of the polar bear kept them warm. The man at left is wearing a pair of pants made of polar bear fur. Modern scientists have not invented a material as warm as this.

Some people in the Arctic still hunt polar bears in the traditional ways of their ancestors. But more often their subsistence hunting is done with snowmobiles instead of dog teams and with guns instead of spears.

According to legend, the polar bear has a spirit that is wise and strong. When a hunter kills a polar bear, he honors its spirit by placing its skull in his window.

Humans and the environment decide the fate of most wild animals. The polar bear is no exception. For 30 years, from the 1940s to the 1970s, it was open season on the polar bear. An animal that had long been hunted with respect and considerable risk by the Inuit was soon being slaughtered from the sky.

Trophy hunting by airplane reduced the risk to the hunter and greatly increased the chances of a kill. In some cases, two planes herded the bear to an appropriate spot for the fatal shot or shots. (It sometimes took as many as 20 shots to fell a polar bear.) In other cases, boxes mounted with guns were baited to attract a bear. When a bear took the bait, it automatically triggered the gun. Polar bears were killed by the hundreds. In Norway, just two hunting groups killed 400 bears. A single Norwegian hunter killed more than 700. When it was reported that polar bears might soon be extinct, the price of skins soared to new heights and prompted more hunting.

Scientists and concerned citizens of several countries convinced their governments to take action on behalf of the polar bear. Reaching agreement between six nations that share the Arctic was not easy. But Canada, the United States, Norway, Russia, Denmark, and Greenland did finally agree. The 1973 Agreement on Conservation of Polar Bears banned hunting from aircraft and large motorized boats. In the United States, the Marine Mammal Protection Act of 1972 offered additional protection. More than 50 countries are required by the Convention on International Trade in Endangered Species (CITES) to maintain records on the import and export of polar bears or their parts. Limited subsistence hunting is allowed by some Arctic nations.

From an estimated low of 5,000 to 10,000 polar bears, the population has increased to about 25,000. Polar bears are classed as vulnerable and conservation dependent. Their future can be stable provided the delicate environmental balance of the Arctic is maintained and oil spills are avoided. Protecting the polar bear means preserving the plants and animals on which it depends — the ringed seals and bearded seals it eats, the fish and crustaceans the seals eat, and the aquatic plant life the fish, mollusks, crabs, and shrimps require.

Greenland is home to the world's largest national park, and other Arctic nations also protect large wilderness areas. In these protected areas, all natural resources—including the polar bear—are being saved for future generations.

Index

Polar Bears

Series Created by
John Bonnett Wexo

Written by
Timothy Levi Biel

Editorial Consultant
John Bonnett Wexo

Scientific Consultants
Dr. Douglas DeMaster
Leader, Marine Mammal Assessment Investigation
National Marine Fisheries Service

Dr. Ian Stirling
Canadian Wildlife Services